HORRIBLE FACTS

Capella

This edition published in 2007 by Arcturus Publishing Limited
26/27 Bickels Yard, 151–153 Bermondsey Street,
London SE1 3HA

In Canada published for Indigo Books
468 King St W,
Suite 500,
Toronto,
Ontario M5V 1L8

ISBN: 978-1-84193-778-6

Printed in China

CONTENTS

Don't try this at home!

There are some pretty yukky things in this book – in fact, some are world records in grossness. But that doesn't mean you should try to out-gross them yourself. Some are really rather dangerous, others are just plain crazy. Would you want to sit in a bath of rattlesnakes or swallow earthworms whole? Of course not! If you discover a snail the size of a cat or grow a beard a long as a bus, get in touch with the Guinness Book of World Records. Otherwise, leave it to the experts.

Body Facts

The acid in your stomach is so strong that it can dissolve steel razor blades – it's still not a good idea to eat them, though!

Egyptian mummies that have been dead for 3,000 years still have their fingerprints intact.

In the old days, children being trained as acrobats for circuses were strapped into strange and often very painful positions to make their bodies more bendy.

Anne Boleyn, one of King Henry VIII's six wives, had six fingers on each hand and an extra nipple. This was claimed to be evidence of witchcraft and was used in her trial when Henry had her executed in 1536.

More than 100 million micro-organisms live in your mouth at any time.

A beef tapeworm, caught from eating eggs in infected beef, can grow to 12 metres (39 feet) long in the human gut.

In 1970, a thief was caught in Zurich, Switzerland, when a finger that had been cut off by broken glass at the crime scene was matched to his finger prints in police records.

The maw-worm can grow to 30 centimetres (1 foot) and then come out of the body from any gap or hole, including the corner of the eye.

You go white when really scared because blood drains from your skin. This protected primitive humans from bleeding to death if bitten by scary, wild animals.

Girls who made matches in the 1800s often suffered from 'phossy jaw' – their jaw bones would rot away, poisoned by the phosphorus used to make the matches.

The average person loses 200 millilitres (7 fluid ounces) of water a day in their faeces.

Long ago, rich people used to pay for teeth to be pulled from poor people – often teenagers – and implanted in their own jaws when their rotten teeth were removed.

More than 200 types of different organisms live inside or on your body at any time.

All the bacteria living inside your body would fill six teaspoons.

In 1973, Italian kidnappers were paid a ransom of over $3 million after they cut off the ear of their kidnap victim and sent it to his very rich grandfather, John Paul Getty.

If you could scrunch together all the bacteria living on the outside of your body, they would take up about the same amount of space as one pea.

If your vomit looks like what you've just eaten, that's exactly what it is. If it's soupy, then it's because it's been in your stomach for a while.

Pinworms cause an itchy bottom because they sneak out at night to lay their eggs there.

When diarrhoea turns pale, it contains bits of the lining of your gut.

Urine doesn't contain bacteria. Becalmed or shipwrecked sailors used to drink it with no ill-effects.

Dentists in the Far East used to pull teeth out with their bare hands! In China, they practised by pulling nails out of wood with their fingers.

Your body needs sleep. Staying awake for two weeks can be enough to kill you.

Adult feet produce about a quarter of a cup of sweat a day from 250,000 pores – wait four days and you could make a cup of foot-sweat tea!

Foods that will make you fart include beans, bran, broccoli, sprouts, cabbage, cauliflower and onions.

The larvae of the pork tapeworm, hatched from eggs eaten in infected pork, can travel around the body and live in the brain, eyes, heart or muscles.

At least 1.3 billion people are infected with a small hookworm that attaches to the inside of the gut. If there are a lot, it looks like fur or a thick carpet. Around the world, they suck a total of 10 million litres (around 21 million pints) of blood a day.

An Indian man known as Snake Manu can put small snakes, including deadly cobras, into his mouth and pass them out through his nose.

In Ancient Mexico, people bound their babies' heads tightly to make their skulls long and thin.

When a wound gets infected, it oozes yellow pus. Pus is a mixture of dead blood cells, bacteria and other dead cells from your body.

Surma girls of Ethiopia put clay disks in their lower lip, stretching the lip outwards. The size of the disk indicates how many cattle a man needs to provide to marry the girl – they can be up to 15 centimetres (6 inches) across.

Prickly heat rash is caused by sweat sticking to the layer of dead skin cells on top of your skin. As the cells can't fall off, the sweat can't escape and makes the live cells underneath swell up.

Most people have mites – very tiny creatures related to spiders – living in their eyelashes, eyebrows, ears and noses.

For a work entitled *Self*, created in 1991, English sculptor Marc Quinn made a copy of his head, moulded from his own deep-frozen blood. Quinn collected almost 4 litres (8 pints) of his blood over five months, poured it into a mould of his head and froze it.

About 70 millilitres (around 2.5 fluid ounces) of blood are spurted out of your heart with each beat.

The wucheria worm can live in the lymph system and grow up to 12 centimetres (5 inches) long.

About a third of your faeces is not old food, but bacteria that help you to digest food, and bits of the lining of the inside of your gut.

In some parts of Africa and on some Pacific islands, people make patterns of raised scars on their skin as a decoration or to show their bravery. The wounds are made with sharp spikes or thorns from plants and often rubbed with special kinds of earth or leaves to created coloured tattoos.

In some countries, the umbilical cord – the cord that attaches the unborn baby to its mother – is dried and kept after birth, to use in spells or medicines.

Pilgrims to the Tirupati temple in India give some of their hair as a sacrifice. The temple employs 600 barbers who work day and night to shave pilgrims, taking 6.5 million gifts of hair a year. The hair is sold to wig-makers and for use as fertilizer.

People who lose an arm or leg in an accident or operation can often still feel it hurting, aching or itching but can do nothing to make it feel better.

Dust mites are found in all houses. They eat the dead skin we shed all the time, and live in beds, carpets, rugs and anywhere else snug which collects flakes of skin.

If you unravelled all the tiny tubes in your kidneys and laid them end to end, they would stretch 80 kilometres (50 miles). Yet they scrunch up to fit into kidneys only 10 centimetres (4 inches) long.

An amoeba common in warm water can travel up your nose while you are swimming and live in your brain, where it multiplies rapidly and kills you in three to seven days.

You will produce 45,000 litres (around 95,000 pints) of urine in your life – enough to fill a small swimming pool!

The old Chinese medical technique of acupuncture involves sticking lots of very thin needles into a person's body. The theory is that putting the needles on 'energy pathways' around the body relieves pain and cures illness.

Urine is a good remedy for jellyfish stings, so if you're standing in the sea and get stung, just urinate down your legs.

Head lice can change colour to merge in with the hair they are hiding in.

Athlete's foot is a fungus that grows in the warm, sweaty spaces between your toes. It causes itching and split skin.

Liposuction is a popular operation in Europe and the USA amongst people who feel they are too fat. A surgeon sticks a long, hollow needle into the fat part – such as the tummy or thighs – uses ultrasound to turn the fat to yellow mush, and then sucks it out through the needle.

The palms of the hands are the sweatiest parts of the body, followed by the feet.

If you don't brush plaque off your teeth, it hardens into a substance called tartar which is like cement and impossible to remove with your toothbrush.

The medical name for ear wax is *cerumen*; it is produced by more than 4,000 glands in your ears.

It's possible to get dandruff in your eyebrows as well as in the hair on top of your head.

Chewing gum and using straws both make you burp more as they encourage you to swallow air.

When Ancient Egyptians mummified someone, they used a special long-handled spoon to scoop the brains out through the dead person's nose. They often fed the brain to animals.

A facelift to remove wrinkles involves cutting away part of the skin, pulling the remainder tight again and stitching it in place.

Some people have injections of collagen to 'plump up' their wrinkles. The collagen – a fibre found in skin – is usually taken from pigs or cows.

If you never wear shoes, the skin on the soles of your feet eventually thickens and hardens so that you can walk over sharp stones without hurting yourself.

The Bedouin people in the Middle East consider it polite to burp after a meal.

Hair grows all over your body except the palms of your hands, soles of your feet and your lips.

A single drop of blood contains 250 million blood cells.

Vomiting a lot can give you a black eye – the pressure can burst the blood vessels around your eyes.

Romans used to clean their teeth with 1e, and it was used as a mouthwash until the 1800s in Europe.

A bruise is bleeding under your skin. The blood can't get out if there isn't a cut, so it just leaks around – it's purple because that's the colour of blood that doesn't have any oxygen in it.

Even a bald person has very fine hair on their head, called *vellus*.

If you could line up all your blood cells – all 25 billion of them – they would go round the world four times.

The medical name for burping is *eructation*.

The gunge that collects in your belly button is a mix of dirt, dead skin cells and oils from your body.

The Binderwur tribe in India used to kill and eat sick and old people to please their goddess Kali.

Your belly button is formed from the shrivelled up stump of the umbilical cord – the tube that connected you to your mother's body before you were born.

Most people fart about 14 times a day.

Over a ton of pubic hair has to be filtered out of London's sewage each year and removed to landfill sites.

At any one time, parasites account for one-hundredth of your body weight.

A very fat person who flushes an aeroplane toilet while still sitting on it can have their rectum sucked out by the pull of the toilet's flush.

Human hair grows about just over a centimetre (half an inch) a month.

Air you swallow, and gas released from food as you digest it, comes out as a burp or a fart – which one depends on how far through your intestines it has got.

Expert botfly squeezers (employed to remove botfly maggots from people) can shoot a botfly from a warble distances over 3 metres (10 feet) or more.

The botfly lays its eggs on a mosquito, and they hatch when the mosquito bites someone. The maggot grows for six weeks in a lump under the persons' skin called a *warble* distances of until it pops out when it's fully grown.

The best recorded distance for projectile vomiting is 8 metres (27 feet)!

When you die, the bacteria in your gut start to eat away at you from the inside.

A man with the stage name of Enigma has had surgery to give him horns on his head. He is hoping to get a tail sometime in the future.

In some parts of the world, people wear extremely heavy ear-rings to weigh their ears down and stretch the lobes. They can weigh up to half a kilogram (1 pound) and hang from huge, long holes in the ear lobe.

Rhinotillexomania is the scientific word for picking your nose.

When you breathe normally, air goes into your nose at about 6.5 kilometres (4 miles) per hour. When you take a good sniff at something, it goes in at 32 kilometres (20 miles) per hour. When you sneeze, it comes out at 160 kilometres (100 miles) per hour!

A scab forms because cells in your blood called platelets make a very thin fibre that traps other blood cells and holds them in a layer that dries out over a scratch or cut.

If you could lay out all your blood vessels end to end they would go round the world over twice.

There is enough iron in the human body to make a nail.

Your body absorbs about two-thirds of the volume of the food you eat – the rest is squished into faeces.

A dead body quickly looks greyish as the blood drains down to the part of the body closest to the ground. The effect is most noticeable in people with white skin.

The mental disorder called 'walking corpse' disease leads people to believe parts of their body are missing or that they are dead.

Hookworms can infest people who walk barefoot. They bore through the skin of the feet and travel in the blood to the lungs, where they come out and crawl up to the throat, to be swallowed and start a new life in the gut.

Right-handed people sweat most under their right arm, left-handed people sweat most under their left arm.

People who live in big cities make more ear wax than those who live in the country, where the air is cleaner.

Thrush is an infection that causes a white, hairy fungus to grow on the tongue.

Nearly half the dust in your house – and what you vacuum up when you clean the house – is old skin cells!

Your intestines are about four times your height – they fit because they're all squashed up and coiled around.

An adult has around 5 million hairs on their head and body.

Nose-pickings are a mix of drying mucus and rubbish filtered out of the air you breathe in – pollen, dust, smoke, dirt, sand, and even tiny particles of dust from space!

The skin of an adult laid out flat on the floor would cover about 1.67 square metres (18 square feet).

Dandruff is a mixture of dirt and dead skin cells stuck together with oil that oozes out of your glands on your head. If your head oozes too much oil, your dandruff becomes noticeable.

Babies can get extra thick, yellow dandruff that sticks to their heads in scales. It's called cradle cap and is more noticeable because they usually don't have much hair.

The toilet paper that Americans use in one day would go around the world nine times.

A person produces 1.5 litres (2.6 pints) of spit (saliva) every day and swallows almost all of it.

You lose 80 hairs from your head every day – but you have about 100,000 so don't worry, you won't start to look bald just yet. And they re-grow quickly when you're young.

> **Your heart pumps around 182 million litres (48 million gallons) of blood in your lifetime – with an endless supply of blood, it could fill a swimming pool in less than a month!**

Beards grow faster than any other body hair. If a man never cut his beard, it would grow 9.1 metres (30 feet) in his lifetime.

> **If you could spread out your lungs on the ground, unravelling all the tiny little pockets, they would cover a tennis court.**

When you sneeze, all your body functions stop – even your heart stops beating. A very long sneezing fit can cause a heart attack.

When you blush, your stomach blushes, too! A blush sends blood flooding into the tiny blood vessels on your face and also to the many blood vessels inside your stomach.

When you vomit, the same muscle movements that push food down through your gut go into reverse, pushing it back up again.

The longest tape worm ever found in a human was 33 metres (around 108 feet long).

It can take up to two days for food to pass through your body – from going in your mouth to coming out your bottom.

A spot or pimple is caused by a waxy oil called *sebum* and tiny bits of dead skin collecting in a little hole in your skin. It goes black if it gets big enough to force your pore open and let air in. When bacteria start to eat away at the gunk, a red spot with nasty yellow pus inside grows.

One in 100,000 people is born with an extra finger on each hand, but usually they are only small stumps.

Roundworm is the most common gut parasite in the world. It looks rather like an earthworm, and you can catch it by eating food contaminated with faeces.

A smelly fart contains the same gas that makes rotten eggs stink – hydrogen sulphide.

If you laid out the airways in your lungs in a long line they would stretch over 2,400 kilometres (1,500 miles).

If too much wax builds up in your ears, a doctor can soften it and then scoop it out with a special spoon called a *curette*.

Danish astronomer Tyco Brahe wore a metal nose because his own fell off after he suffered from the disease *syphilis*.

Sometimes, if a person's eye comes out of its socket in an accident and dangles on their cheek, they can push it back in with no lasting ill effects – don't try it at home!

Science Facts

Many tribes around the world have practised trepanning since the Stone Age. It involves drilling a hole in the skull, often with a stone, to ease headaches by letting out evil spirits. People frequently survived, as many skulls have been found with several such holes, some partially healed.

In 1962, a Dutch doctor decided to try trepanning. He used an electric drill to make a hole in his own head.

Malaria is a deadly disease spread by mosquitoes. It is caused by a tiny parasite that lives inside a person's blood cells. Malaria kills 1–3 million people a year.

Early Indian surgeons used ants to hold the edges of wounds together. They would get an ant to bite through both sides of the wound, then twist off the ant's body and throw it away, leaving the head in place with the jaws acting as a stitch.

Railway workers in France in the 1800s claimed to have freed a Pterodactyl trapped in rock. They said it flapped, squawked and died. Reports of frogs and other animals trapped in solid rock are quite common, but not scientifically proven.

If you fell into a black hole you would be stretched into an incredibly long, thin string in a process called 'spaghettification'.

Snake venom is not normally poisonous if swallowed because stomach acid alters the chemicals in it.

A toxin in the nectar of laurels and rhododendrons makes honey made from these plants poisonous. In 66 BCE, Roman troops were lured by their enemies into a grove where bees made honey from these flowers. The soldiers ate it and were slaughtered while sick.

The scientific name for a fear of peanut butter sticking to the roof of your mouth is *arachibutyrophobia*.

Cells taken from the inside of baby teeth when they fall out have been grown and have reproduced in the laboratory. Put into the jaws of mice, they grow into soft teeth, with no hard enamel on the outside.

Urine contains chemicals that we use in cleaning fluids and used to be used for cleaning things.

There are 'banks' where the umbilical cords of new babies can be stored in case future medical developments make it possible to grow new organs or tissues from cells in them.

Scientists investigating tumour growth added a gene from a firefly to make a glow-in-the-dark tumour. The tumour is visible through the skin of a test animal, so scientists can see if it grows or shrinks.

> **Some animals respond to small amounts of poisonous gas and have been used as early warning systems. German soldiers kept cats in the trenches of the First World War to smell gas, and British miners kept budgies in cages because they died quickly if gas escaped into the mine.**

A fear of worms is called *scoleciphobia*.

There are over 20,000 road crashes involving kangaroos in Australia every year, so a robo-roo robotic test crash dummy like a kangaroo is used to test how badly cars will be damaged.

> **A person would need to weigh around 650 kilograms (1,433 pounds) to have enough fat to stop a bullet. Although their body would be bullet-proof, they could still be killed by a shot to the head.**

In 1999, an artist in Chicago, USA, announced his plan to grow a glow-in-the-dark dog by adding a gene from jellyfish to it.

Victorian children were often given their own salt cellar, which they were told was a sign of being grown up. In fact, the salt was mixed with *bromide*, which made them calmer and better behaved.

Police scientists investigating a murder can work out how long a body ha[s] been dead by looking at th[e] kinds of maggots, worms an[d] insects that are eating it.

Potatoes, aubergines, tomatoes and peppers all belong to the same family of plants as deadly nightshade!

Scientists are working on a microscopic robotic tadpole to deliver medicines – the tadpole would 'swim' through the patient's blood vessels to take the medicine where it's needed.

Not all dead bodies rot. In the right conditions, some of the fat can turn to a soap-like substance so that if the body is dug up, even years later, it can look much the same as when it was buried.

Archaeologists find out about what people in the Stone Age ate by examining Stone Age faeces called *coprolites*. They have to be soaked in water for three days first to soften them.

An unusual form of drug abuse is licking cane toads. They make a slime containing a drug which produces hallucinations (strange experiences or visions). People in some parts of Australia and the USA have started licking the toads to enjoy the drug.

Fake mermaids made from bits of monkey and fish have been produced to fool scientists for years – most recently with one claimed to have been washed up by the tsunami in Asia in 2004. The oldest so-called mummified mermaid is 1,400 years old and from Japan.

Australian Benjamin Drake Van Wissen invented machinery to mine guano on the Pacific island of Nauru and turn it into fertilizer.

Green potatoes contain a poison, *solanin*, which can be deadly. It develops in old potatoes that are not kept in the dark. Eating 2 kilograms (4.4 pounds) of green potatoes could be fatal.

If you are trapped in snow in an avalanche, it's impossible to tell which way is up (and so which way to dig yourself out). Urinate and see which direction the yellow stain spreads – gravity will pull the urine down.

Oil is made from the decayed bodies of animals and plants that died millions of years ago and have been squashed deep underground.

In 1822, Dr. William Beaumont studied human digestion as it happened, through a hole in the side and stomach of a patient who had been shot. The hole did not heal, allowing Dr. Beaumont to study it, but also allowing food and drink to ooze out if it was not covered up.

In an attempt to kill malaria-carrying mosquitoes, an American scientist built towers to attract bats. He enticed them in with fabric covered with bat droppings, and played music near the bats' old homes to drive them out. After a few years, malaria infection dropped from 89 percent of the population to zero.

The most poisonous metal in the world is arsenic. It used to be made into fly papers for killing flies, but it killed some people, too.

If you cut spinach with an iron knife, both will go black as a chemical in the spinach reacts with the iron.

During the First World War, goldfish were used to check whether all traces of poisonous gas had been washed out of gas masks. The mask was rinsed and filled with water, then a goldfish was dropped in. If it died, there was still gas left in it.

Around 1,400 years ago, the Chinese used to make gunpowder by boiling up and burning pig manure. To make sure it was ready, and not polluted with salt, they licked the crystals.

> **People used to use white lead powder to make their skin look white and beautiful, but it gave them lead poisoning and slowly killed them. As their skin looked worse once the poison took effect, they used more white lead to cover up the damage.**

It can take a hundred years for the body of a whale at the bottom of the sea to disappear completely, as it is slowly eaten away by different animals, plants and microbes.

> **Early matches were made of poisonous chemicals and would sometimes burst into flames on their own if they got warm and damp. They poisoned the children employed to make them, and set fire to people's pockets unexpectedly!**

A small animal such as a mouse can be dropped 1,000 metres (3,280 feet) down a mineshaft and suffer no harm because the fastest speed it can fall it is not enough to crush its body. The larger an animal or object, the shorter the distance it can safely fall.

Scraping mould off your food doesn't get rid of it – behind the fuzzy part you can see, strings extend into the food up to nine times the length of the visible part.

Our blood is red because it uses an iron compound to carry oxygen – some spiders have blue blood because theirs uses a copper compound instead.

John Haigh killed six people in London, UK, in the 1940s, dissolving their bodies in a bath of acid, hoping he could wash away all the evidence. However, on finding three human gallstones and a pair of dentures belonging to one of his victims in the sludge left behind, the police had enough evidence to convict him.

Old cannonballs brought up from the seabed can explode and kill divers. Bacteria eat away part of the metal, producing gases that rapidly expand when the cannonballs come to the surface.

A medieval cure for stammering was scalding the tongue with a red-hot iron. It didn't work...

If you draw pictures in the condensation on a window, the picture will reappear next time the window mists over as a layer of grease from your skin stays on the glass and repels the water.

Earthworms bring 4 million kilograms (8.8 million pounds) of earth to the surface on every square kilometre (0.38 square miles) of open ground each year.

In the 1600s, spiders rolled in butter were recommended as a cure for malaria.

There have been several recorded cases of spontaneous human combustion (people who apparently burst into flames for no good reason). Sometimes, all that is left is a burnt patch and perhaps a foot or some singed clothing.

Rats trained to look for landmines are so light that they don't trigger the mechanism if they tread on one. Instead, they scratch and bite at the ground when they smell explosives, and the handler deals with the mine.

If you fall off a very high cliff or building, the fastest speed you will ever fall at is around 200 kilometres (124 miles) per hour. This is called terminal velocity, and it's enough to make a nasty splat.

Horses killed in the First World War were recycled as explosives – their fat was removed and boiled down to be used in making TNT.

Bird droppings are the main export of the island Nauru in the western Pacific Ocean. They're used for fertilizer, as they're rich in the chemical nitrogen.

Scientists believe that all vertebrates (animals with backbones) evolved from giant tadpoles, 6 centimetres (2.5 inches) long, that swam around 550 million years ago.

Some wealthy people have their bodies *cryopreserved* (deep-frozen) when they die, in the hope that in the future someone will find a cure for their cause of death and resurrect them. The popular urban legend that Walt Disney was cryopreserved is false; he was cremated.

It is so cold in space, that urine flushed out of a space craft instantly freezes into a stream of yellow crystals.

A man who experimented with feeding a Venus flytrap – a type of flesh-eating plant – with bits of his own flesh found the plant could digest it easily. He used bits of his toes that had rotted and dropped off as a result of athlete's foot.

If potatoes were discovered today, they would probably be banned under European Union regulations as too dangerous.

The chemical phosphorous was discovered by German chemist Hening Brandt in 1669. He made it by leaving urine to rot and then heating it until the liquid evaporated.

There are 100 million times more insects than people on earth and their total weight is 12 times the total weight of people.

In an emergency, coconut milk can be used as substitute for the watery part of blood in a blood transfusion.

Lined up neatly, 10,000 bacteria would stretch across your thumbnail.

Japanese scientists have managed to grow tadpole eyes from scratch in the laboratory. They transplanted the eyes into tadpoles. The eyes worked even after the tadpoles changed into frogs.

The average bed is home to 6 million dust mites.

Ergot is fungus that grows on rye and causes people to act as though mad if they eat it. Some historians think that people accused of witchcraft who said they could fly, or those who accused others of strange, magical behaviour, may have had ergot poisoning.

The germs present in faeces can pass through 10 layers of toilet paper – that's why you need to wash your hands!

The largest living thing in the world is a fungus in Washington state, USA, which covers 6.5 square kilometres (2.5 square miles) and has been growing for hundreds of years.

The Masai tribe in Africa drink cow or bull urine as a sedative (drug to calm people down or make them sleepy).

There is a cockroach museum in Plano, Texas.

Some people – most of them in the USA – claim that they have been abducted by aliens from space while they slept, had their bodies experimented on and sometimes their minds changed, and were then returned to Earth.

It's said that dead Americans rot much more slowly than they used to – because they eat so many preservatives in their foods.

A will-o'-the-wisp is a flame of burning marsh gas that appears in boggy areas at night. It has lured many travellers to a muddy death when they have left the path to follow it, believing it to be someone with a light.

The castor bean plant contains the most deadly poison in the natural world, ricin. Just 70 micrograms (2-millionths of an ounce) could kill an adult human. It is 12,000 times more poisonous than rattle snake venom!

Bacteria – tiny living things that we also call germs – divide in two every 20 minutes. So, starting with one (it doesn't need a girlfriend/boyfriend), you can have over 130 million in just 9 hours!

The average glass of London tap water has passed through nine people's bladders before it reaches your sink.

Some scientists think that being too clean might make us ill – some studies suggest that people need to eat a small amount of dirt in order to kick start their immune systems. Not learning to fight infections can lead to asthma and other allergic problems.

One possible way of controlling cockroaches being explored in the USA is to release parasitic worms which will kill the roaches but don't harm people.

The stinking corpse plant, or *rafflesia*, is a huge parasitic flower that smells like rotting meat. The flower is up to a metre (about 3 feet) across and is the largest flower in the world. It grows directly out of a creeping vine, from which it gains all its nourishment without ever growing leaves of its own.

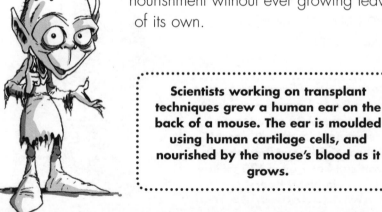

Scientists working on transplant techniques grew a human ear on the back of a mouse. The ear is moulded using human cartilage cells, and nourished by the mouse's blood as it grows.

Deodorants don't stop you sweating but they kill the bacteria that make sweat smell.

A cure for whooping cough used in Yorkshire, England in the 1800s was to drink a bowl of soup with nine frogs hidden in it. You couldn't make it yourself – it only worked if you didn't know about the frogs. (And probably not then, either!)

A Roman cure for epilepsy (having fits) was to bathe in the blood of a gladiator.

Romans dressed small wounds with spider webs soaked in vinegar.

The earliest study of brain damage was of railway worker Phineas Gage. In 1848, an explosion shot a thick iron rod through his head. Although he recovered physically, his character changed completely. His skull and the iron rod are on display in Harvard University, USA.

People on the Pacific island of Chuuk use a love potion made from centipede's teeth and stingray tails.

For centuries, it was illegal to cut up dead bodies, so surgeons and scientists had to pay criminals to steal the corpses of executed prisoners from the gallows in order to learn about anatomy.

An old cure for tuberculosis consisted of cutting open a newly dead cow, pulling the folds of skin around your neck and breathing in deeply.

Air conditioning systems are home to lots of nasty bacteria. And because they pump the same air around a building again and again, they are one of the best ways of spreading diseases to everyone in the building.

A chemical extracted from leeches is used as a painkiller.

Food Facts

Bedouin wedding feasts sometimes include a roast camel, stuffed with a sheep, stuffed with chickens, stuffed with fish, stuffed with eggs.

> **Henry V of England once held a Christmas feast at which the menu included carps' tongues, roasted dolphin and flowers set in jelly.**

In the 1800s, it was common to mix ground bones into flour to make it go further.

An average-sized person eats around 22,700 kilograms (50,000 pounds) of food over the course of their life.

> **Honey is bee vomit. Bees drink nectar from flowers which they turn into honey before sicking it back up to store in the hive.**

The Roman emperor Nero kept a 'glutton' – an Egyptian slave who ate everything he was given to eat, including human flesh.

Flavours of ice-cream available in Japan include octopus, ox tongue, cactus, chicken wing and crab.

To make especially tender beef, the Japanese shut cattle in the dark, feed them beer and employ special cattle masseurs to massage them by hand three times a day.

Stink-heads are a traditional Alaskan dish. Fish heads – often from salmon – are buried in pits lined with moss for a few weeks or months until rotten. They are then kneaded like pastry to mix up all the parts and eaten.

Argentinian Gauchos keep a piece of beef under their saddles so that it is pummelled until tender as they ride around all day. It's said that the dish steak tartar came from Mongolian warriors doing the same and then eating the steak raw.

The Spanish eat the cheese *cabrales* when it is 'con gusano' – crawling with live maggots.

In India, ants are roasted, ground to a paste and served as chutney.

In Sardinia, cheese is left in the sun for flies to lay their egg in. When the maggots hatch, th swarming mass is spread on bread and eaten.

An eighteenth-century recipe for making an enormous egg suggests sewing 20 egg yolks into an animal bladder, then dropping it into another animal bladder filled with 20 egg whites and boiling it all together.

A stew eaten at a funeral in Stone-Age Wales was made from shellfish, eels, mice, frogs, toads, shrews and snakes.

In 1919, a tidal wave of treacle swept through Boston, USA. A storage tank burst, spilling 7.5 million litres (2 million gallons) of it into the streets. It poured over houses, knocking them down, in a wave two storeys high.

During the Second World War, people in the UK were urged by the government to make the most of wild foods, and were given recipes for cooking roast squirrel, rook casserole, stewed starlings and baked sparrows.

In 1971, a man found the head of a mouse in a bar of chocolate.

Odd crisp flavours available around the world include octopus, seaweed, banana, and sour cream and squid.

Condemned prisoners are traditionally allowed a delicious last meal. In some US states, it's not actually their last meal, but is served a day or two before the execution and is called a 'special meal'.

The Insect Club, a restaurant in the USA, serves only dishes made with insects. The menu includes cricket pizza, insect chocolates and 'insects in a blanket' – crickets, mealworms and blue cheese in puff pastry.

Tradition tells that the French cheese Roquefort was discovered when a shepherd abandoned his lunch in a cave to chase a pretty girl he saw outside. When he came back months later the cheese had gone mouldy but still tasted good.

> **Roman banquets often featured hummingbirds cooked in walnut shells and roasted stuffed dormice, sometimes rolled in honey and poppy seeds. The Romans even had farms producing dormice because they were so popular.**

Durian is a fruit the size of a football, covered in spikes, that smells like rotting meat. It's supposed to taste good, though!

In Slovenia, people still raise and fatten dormice, ready to stew.

In Nepal, Tibet and parts of China, black tea is served with yak butter – butter made from yak milk.

> **During the First World War, Germany suffered such food shortages that people ate dogs and horses, and even the kangaroos from the zoos!**

Raake orret is eaten in Norway. Trout caught in a fresh water stream are stored in salted water with a little sugar and kept in a cool place, such as the garage, for months before eating.

P'tcha is an east European Jewish food made by stewing calves' feet until they turn to jelly.

Ambuyat, eaten in Brunei, is made from pulp from the sago palm, stewed in water for several hours. The same mixture is made to stick the roof on a house!

In Northern Australia, children often eat green ants. Pick them up, squish the head so they don't nibble you, and bite off the body.

Also in Brunei, the sago worm which lives inside rotting sago palms is often cooked and eaten.

In Madagascar, people make a stew from tomatoes and zebras.

Pruno is a 'wine' made by American prisoners from a mixture of fruit, sugar cubes, water and tomato ketchup left to fester in a bin bag for a week. In some prisons, pruno causes so many discipline problems that fruit has been banned.

A restaurant in Osaka, Japan, serve whale ice-cream made from the blubber of the minke whale.

In the Japanese countryside, salamanders and skinks are grilled on sticks and served with lettuce.

In Nicaragua, turtle eggs are eaten raw – slit the leathery skin, add some hot sauce and suck out the gunk.

Cinemas in Colombia serve paper cones filled with giant fried or toasted ants.

A rat restaurant in China sells rat and snake soup, rat kebabs, steamed rat with rice and crispy fried rat.

In Newfoundland, Canada, seal flipper pie is a traditional dish for the end of a seal hunt.

A restaurant in Changsha, China, offers food cooked in human breast milk.

Think cabbage is horrid? In Korea, it is sometimes buried in clay pots with salt for many months before it's eaten – this dish is called kimchi, and is served with most meals.

Alligator kebabs are popular in southern Louisiana, USA.

In Fiji, people starve a pig for a week, then feed it veal when it is very hungry. A few hours later, they kill the pig and remove the half-digested veal, which they cook and eat.

In Texas, there's an annual rattle-snake round-up. What to do with all the rattle snakes? Skin them, gut them, cut them into chunks, cover in batter and deep fry.

Another way of cooking snakes in Texas – cut the head off, skin and gut it, poke a stick into the neck, wrap the snake loosely around the stick and roast over a camp fire.

In China, people eat jellied ducks' blood.

Iguanas are a popular and free food in Central America – they can often be caught in backyards.

> **Slimy green stuff that looks like mucus is supposedly the best part of a lobster or crayfish. It's found in the head. Some Americans eat the main part of the lobster meat and then suck the head to get the gunge out.**

As early as the ninth century, the Basques of Spain hunted whales, and whale tongue was considered a great delicacy.

Oellebroed is a Danish soup make from stale rye bread soaked in water, then boiled with beer and sugar and served with cream. It's possible to buy instant oellebroed powder – just add water.

Cibreo is an Italian dish that consists of the cooked combs from roosters.

Spam is a luncheon meat used as a filling for sandwiches. At a Spam-cooking contest, one contestant made Spam-chip cookies!

Baby mouse wine, from China, is a bottle of wine packed with baby mice, to add flavour.

In Canada, deep-fried cod tongues are a popular dish.

The street markets of Indonesia sell whole, smoked bats.

McDonald's in Hong Kong sells a sweetcorn pie in a sweet pie crust, the same as the apple pies in the west.

An international contest to find the best recipe for cooking earthworms included entries of stews, salads and soups but was won by a recipe for applesauce surprise cake. Guess what the surprise was…

Jack Fuller was buried in a pyramid in Sussex, England, in 1811. It's said by local people that inside it he is seated at a table with a roast chicken and a bottle of port.

Some Arctic explorers have been poisoned by eating polar bear liver. The polar bear eats so much fish that fatal levels of Vitamin D collect in its liver.

The Chinese make a soup from the swim bladder of fish. It's the organ that helps fish to stay at the right depth and upright in the water, and is rather spongy.

A restaurant in Pennsylvania, USA, offers a hamburger that weighs 4 kilograms (9 pounds). No one has yet managed to finish one.

Drunken shrimps, served in China, are live shrimps swimming in a bowl of rice wine. The idea is to catch them with chopsticks and bite the heads off.

In Ness, Scotland, people kill young gannets – a type of sea bird – to eat. The claws are the most highly prized part.

Bedouin people cook a camel's hump by burying it underground and lighting a fire over the top of it. When they dig it up and eat it, the top is cooked, but the bottom still mostly raw and bloody.

Crispy fried duck or chicken feet are a delicacy in China. In the USA, whole chicken feet are sometimes pickled or made into soup.

Eskimos have been known to make seagull wine – put a seagull in a bottle of water, wait for it to go off – drink!

In both Sicily and Japan, people eat the raw roe (eggs) of sea urchins.

In the Philippines, the eyes are considered the tastiest part of a steamed fish. Suck out the gloop and spit out the hard cornea.

Fried chicken cartilage is served as a bar snack in Japan.

Snake wine in China is a very potent alcoholic drink, spiced with juice from the gall bladder of a live snake.

Marmite, a favourite English spread for toast, is made with the left-over yeasty sludge from brewing beer.

In Wales, rook pie was considered a tasty way to get rid of a bird that might otherwise eat the crops.

A traditional dish in London is eels boiled and served cold in jelly.

Nutria are a large rodent that live some of the time in the water. They are a pest in Louisiana, where local authorities are encouraging people to eat them – with little success, as they don't taste too good.

> **In the southern USA, squirrel brains are cooked still in the head. You then crack the skull and scoop the brains out with fingers and fork.**

In Hungary, scrambled eggs are fried up with the blood from a freshly slaughtered pig.

Some prisoners have big appetites. Richard Beavers, executed in Texas in 1994, ate for his last meal: 6 pieces of French toast with butter and syrup, 6 barbecued spare ribs, 6 pieces of bacon (burnt), 4 scrambled eggs, 5 sausage patties, French fries with ketchup, 3 slices of cheese, 2 pieces of yellow cake with chocolate fudge icing and 4 cartons of milk.

Biltong is favoured as a snack by rugby supporters in South Africa. It's dried strips of any meat – elephant, eland, antelope…

In Indonesia, deep fried monkey toes are eaten by sucking the meat straight off the bone.

In Sweden, people make dumplings from flour, reindeer blood and salt.

In Japan, the blowfish is a delicacy, even though it contains a poison gland which, if not properly removed, kills anyone who eats it.

An omelette costing $1000 (£530) and called the Zillion Dollar Lobster Frittata was sold by a restaurant in New York. It contains a whole lobster and 280 grams (10 ounces) of caviar, as well as eggs, cream, potato and whiskey.

In Georgia, there is a price limit of $20 on the last meal a prisoner can order.

Small songbirds cooked and eaten whole have been so popular in Italy that many types have been wiped out completely.

In Sweden and Norway, roast reindeer is a national dish.

Jellyfish are eaten dried and salted in some parts of the world. And in the Gilbert Islands, jellyfish ovaries are served fried.

> **Many cheap meat products such as sausages and burgers are made from 'mechanically recovered meat' which consists of a meat slurry collected from washing bones and mincing up parts of the dead animal that aren't used for anything else.**

In the Philippines, chicken heads may be made into stew or barbecued whole.

Aztecs gave people who were to be human sacrifices many last meals – they fattened them up for up to a year.

The Russian Jewish dish kishke is made by stuffing a chicken skin with flour, butter and spices and boiling it in chicken stock. Dry it out, then cut it into slices as a snack.

The reproductive organs of sea urchins are eaten raw in many parts of the world, including Japan, Chile and France.

In China and Japan, sheets of dried jellyfish are sold for soaking and turning back into slimy jellyfish ready for cooking.

Ancient Greeks, Egyptians and Romans all gave condemned prisoners a last meal.

The town of Bunol, in Spain, has an annual tomato fight when up to 25,000 people throw around 100 tonnes (220,000 pounds) of tomatoes at each other. The streets can be flooded up to 30 centimetres (12 inches) deep with juice.

The Chinese eat monster barnacles the size of an adult's fist.

The alcoholic drink *mescal* has a cactus maggot preserved in the bottle.

In the Samoan Islands, the intestines of sea cucumbers are sold in jars, steeped in sea water. The sea cucumber is a slithery, tube-like animal and not a cucumber at all. When it's cooked, it is called a sea slug.

In the UK, game – wild animals and birds shot in the fields – is often hung until it is 'high', which means it is hung up on a hook until it is starting to go off.

In the Masai Mara in Africa people drink blood drained from the neck of a live animal with a straw, mixed up with milk.

Yeast are tiny fungi (mould), present in bread, beer and wine. The yeast eat sugar in the ingredients, making the gas which forms the bubbles in beer and wine and the holes in bread.

Raw, pickled jellyfish are eaten in the Samoan Islands.

Eels are sold live in markets around the world and killed just before cooking – or before putting in the bag to go home, if you don't want the bag wriggling all the way.

Orangutan lips used to be a delicacy in Vietnam.

The British black pudding is a sausage made of congealed pigs' blood with lumps of fat embedded in it. It is often fried and eaten for breakfast.

Soft ice-cream of the type sold in ice-cream vans is given its slithery smoothness by an extract of seaweed.

Baby eels, called elvers, are eaten in parts of Europe, including east England. They are very thin, so lots are cooked, tangled together like spaghetti.

In France, calves' eyes are soaked in water, then boiled and stuffed and finally deep fried in breadcrumbs.

Most US states don't allow alcohol or tobacco in a prisoner's last meal.

To make the expensive *pate de foie gras*, geese are forcibly fattened with grain so that their liver swells to many times its natural size.

Cow's tongue is often sold with the salivary glands – the parts that make spit – ready for boiling. The tongue can weigh up to 2.3 kilograms (5 pounds).

In Europe, some people make blood pudding from the blood of a pig or cow mixed with rice, milk and sugar and then baked.

In Mexico, the alcoholic drink tequila is often served with a worm in the glass – the worm should be swallowed whole with the drink.

Romany people in Europe, and poor peasants, used to cook wild hedgehogs by rolling them in mud and baking them in the embers of a fire. When the mud dries, the spines can be peeled off with the mud.

In England, lampreys – a fierce fish that looks like an eel – a traditionally cooked in a sauce flavoured with their own blood.

History Facts

In France in the late 1600s, it was considered a great honour to talk to King Louis XIV while he was on the lavatory.

In Anglo-Saxon times, shepherds were given twelve days' worth of cow manure at Christmas.

Vikings used rancid butter to style and dress their hair.

Biological warfare has been used since 600 BCE when the Greek city Cirrha was besieged by Solon. He poisoned the water supply with hellebore roots and stormed the city while the citizens had diarrhoea.

During the 900 days of the siege of Leningrad in the Second World War, 1,500 people were accused of cannibalism.

In Palestine 8–9,000 years ago, a dead relative was buried under the floor of the family's house – except the head. The flesh and brain were removed from the head and the skull used as the base for a plaster mould of the person's head, which was decorated and kept.

The Greeks played the game knucklebones with real bones from the knuckles of animals that have cloven feet – like pigs, goats and antelopes.

After a massacre carried out by Indian soldiers in 1857, the British soldiers made the Indians clean up the blood – and those who refused had to lick it up.

Slaves sometimes had to fight to the death in a Roman arena. To make sure they weren't just pretending to be dead, they could be prodded with a red-hot poker and hit on the head with a huge hammer.

Theban king Mithradites (132–63 BCE) took small doses of poison regularly to develop immunity and protect himself from poisoners. When he later wanted to kill himself, the poison he took did not kill him.

In Sparta, Greece, in 600 b[...] the law required that a [...] born imperfect – disabl[...] deformed – be kille[...] immediately.

Wig-makers suffered during times of plague as people thought the disease could be caught from wigs made of human hair. So many second-hand wigs were infested with fleas that they were probably right!

Toad-eaters were people employed by men selling medicine at fairs and markets. The toad-eater had to swallow a toad – supposed to be deadly poisonous – and then take the medicine. Their survival encouraged people to buy the medicine. They may or may not have actually swallowed the toads…

In Ancient Egypt, women kept a cone of grease on their head. During the day, it melted in the hot sun and dripped down, making their hair gleam with grease.

Birching was allowed as a punishment in Britain until the 1940s. It consisted of being beaten on the bare buttocks with a bunch of twigs.

Victorian child chimney sweeps sometimes had to crawl through chimneys as narrow as 18 centimetres (7 inches). If they didn't go quickly enough, their bare feet were pricked with burning straws.

In the 1990s, fashionable women in Europe who wanted to look thin wore corsets laced so tightly that their ribs were sometimes broken!

In the nineteenth century, a school headmaster in York, England, massacred his pupils and hid their bodie in cupboards.

During the Great Plague that struck England in 1665–66, boys at Eton school were punished for not smoking – smoking was thought to protect them from the disease.

In 1856, the USA passed a law saying that its citizens could claim any uninhabited island anywhere in the world if it contained large deposits of bird faeces.

Mary Stuart, queen of England from 1553 to 1558, had 274 people burned at the stake just for being Protestant Christians.

Pope Clement II tried eating a death cap toadstool in 1534; it killed him.

Before written or computerized records helped us to keep track of criminals, many countries marked criminals with a tattoo or a branding iron – a red hot iron used to burn a pattern, letter or picture into their skin. This meant that everyone could see what they had done.

Bird faeces called guano were collected and sold from Peru, Chile and Bolivia for hundreds of years. It was used as a fertilizer for plants.

The Greek emperor Draco died when he was smothered by the hats and cloaks that admirers threw over him at a party.

A common way of attacking a besieged castle or city in the Middle Ages was to catapult dead animals, corpses or even the heads of enemies over the walls.

It took over two months to make an Egyptian mummy. After removing the internal organs and brain, the body was covered with a kind of salt for two months to dry out, then treated with resin, packed with sand and sawdust and wrapped in bandages.

Mongol leader Tamerlane the Great (1336 –1405) executed anyone who told him a joke he had already heard.

Roman prisoners condemned to fight to death with each other or wild animals often tried to kill themselves before the fight. One man pushed a wooden spike down his throat – it was used for holding the sponge people cleaned themselves with in the lavatory.

In 2,350 BCE the Mesopotamian king Urukagina demanded that thieves be stoned to death with stones carved with their crime.

Anglo-Saxon peasants sometimes wove clothes made out of dried stinging nettles.

> **Anyone who rebelled against the Mesopotamian king Ashurnasirpal could expect to be skinned or buried alive. We know this because he buried some rebels inside a column and carved the story of their crime on the outside.**

In Ancient Rome, vestal virgins were young girls who served in a temple and could not be touched. If they committed a crime their punishment was to be buried alive as it could be done without anyone touching them.

> **The Romans had criminals torn apart by wild animals while the public watched. Dogs or lions were usually used, but sometimes more exotic animals were brought in.**

In the time of King Charles II of England, who reigned from 1649 to 1685, dead people had to buried in a shroud made of wool, to boost business for the wool trade.

The scarab beetle was treated as holy by t Ancient Egyptians. Sca beetles roll themselves in ball of faeces and lay the eggs in it.

In Anglo-Saxon England, people who died in a famine were eaten by their neighbours!

In 1740, a cow found guilty of witchcraft was hanged.

The Roman king Tarquin crucified anyone who committed suicide – even though they were already dead – to show other people what would happen to their bodies if they did the same.

A medieval trial of guilt required a suspected criminal to plunge their hand into a pan of hot water and take out a stone, or carry a red-hot iron bar. The injured arm was bandaged and inspected after three days. If it was healedthe person was considered innocent. If not, they were guilty and were punished.

In 167 BCE, a Roman commander had a group of soldiers trampled to death by elephants for deserting (running away from battle).

Lord Nelson
(1758–1805)
Admiral of the English fleet, left in a coffin in his cabin. The coffin was made from the mast of an enemy French ship.

The Spanish Inquisition was set up to find people who committed crimes against the church and its teachings. They often questioned and tortured people until they confessed. In the case of a child under 10, though, they could go straight to the torture and not bother with the questions.

The Mongolian ruler Ghengis Khan imposed the death penalty for urinating in water because water was so precious in the Mongolian desert.

During the time of Henry VIII of England, who reigned from 1508 to 1547, the punishment for poisoners was to be boiled alive.

To make violin strings, the gut of a sheep – which could be 30 metres long (over 98 feet) in length – was removed intact. The blood, flesh and fat were then scraped off the outside, the half-digested grass was squeezed out and it was washed out carefully.
The wider end was used as sausage skins, the rest for violin strings.

In India, people used to believe that the eyes from a slow lorris – a nocturnal creature like a monkey with no tail – could work as a love potion.

An Ancient Egyptian cure for burns involved warming a frog in goat dung and applying it to the burn.

The Roman emperor Valerian was captured by visigoths (a barbaric tribe) invading Rome in 260 CE, who skinned him alive and then displayed the skin as a signal of their triumph.

When Sir Walter Ralegh was executed in 1618, his wife had his head embalmed. She carried it around with her for 29 years, until her own death.

Ancient Greeks used to blow up a pig's bladder like a balloon and use it as a ball.

An Anglo-Saxon cure for ldness was to rub the ash from burnt bees into the head.

Soldiers fighting in the trenches in World War I often suffered from trench foot (spending too long in cold, wet trenches made their feet rot). Some had to have their feet amputated because of it...

The Hungarian countess Elizabeth Bathori killed more than 600 young girls in the 1500s in order to drink and bathe in their blood.

A French medieval torture involved trapping a person in the stocks – a wooden structure that held their ankles while they sat on the ground – pouring salt water over their bare feet and letting a goat lick it off.

The servants of a dead Egyptian pharaoh were often killed and buried with him or sealed alive in his pyramid.

The poet Shelley drowned off the coast of Italy in 1822. His body was washed up, half eaten by fish, and cremated on the beach by his friends. One of them cut his heart from the burnt body and gave it to Shelley's wife who kept it all her life.

Hanging, drawing and quartering was a punishment for the worst crimes in England from 1241. The prisoner was nearly strangled by hanging, then cut open and had his innards removed and cooked in front of him, and finally chopped into four pieces. By the mid-1700s, prisoners were killed before the drawing and quartering.

Monks in Sicily, Italy, mummified dead bodies until 1920. A display of 6,000 can be seen in catacombs in Palermo, standing around or lying on shelves.

A Saxon cure for madness was a beating with a whip made from the skin of a dolphin.

Ancient Egyptians sometimes brought a mummified body to banquets to remind diners that one day they would die.

Early Colonists in America used to clean their windows with rags dipped in urine.

In the Middle Ages, butchers often killed animals for meat in their shops, then threw the innards out into the street.

Romans who killed a relative would be executed by being tied in a sack with a live dog, cockerel, snake and monkey and thrown into a river.

Fashionable women in Japan and Vietnam stained their teeth black until the mid-1900s.

Wool used to be softened by people trampling on it in a large vat of stale (two-week-old) urine and ground clay. The people who did this were called 'fullers'.

During a famine and drought in Jamestown, America, 1609, one settler was executed for eating his dead wife.

A dead body found in the Alps in 1991 was at first thought to be a climber who had died. Investigators discovered it was a man who had been mummified naturally in the ice after dying 5,300 years ago. They named him Otzi.

So many people associated with the discovery of Otzi have died young that some believe the mummy is cursed.

The Incas of South America used to mummify their dead kings and leave them sitting on their thrones.

People hunting animals examine the faeces of their quarry to find out information about the size, sex and type of animal. In the Middle Ages, hunters often carried the faeces around with them while they hunted, storing them in their hunting horn.

The French actress Sarah Bernhard took a coffin with her on her travels. She learned lines while lying in the coffin and even entertained her lovers in it.

In the 1700s, people wore huge hairstyles made of a mixture of real hair and horse hair or other fibres. As they rarely cleaned them – keeping them in place for months on end– they carried sticks to knock vermin out of their hair-does.

Queen Christina of Sweden, who reigned from 1640 to 1654, had a miniature cannon and crossbow for executing fleas.

Sailors in the olden days often had a single gold tooth, which could be pulled out and used to pay for their funeral if they died away from home.

An Egyptian mummy can have more than 20 layers of bandages, with glue between the layers. Every finger and toe was wrapped separately. It took 15 days to wrap a royal mummy.

Ancient Romans made hair dye from pigeon faeces.

Uruguay's rugby team was stranded in the Andes in South America after a plane crash in 1979. It took seventy days for them to be rescued, and they had to eat the other passengers who had died in the crash.

An Ancient Egyptian who was feeling a bit unwell might eat a mixture of mashed mouse and faeces. Mmmmmmm, bound to make you feel better!

In 1846, eighty-seven pioneers crossing the mountains of Nevada, USA, became trapped in bad weather. By the end of the winter, forty of them had been eaten by the others.

In the 1800s, flea circuses were popular – the fleas were glued into costumes and stuck to wires or each other to look as though they were performing tricks.

King Pepi II of Egypt had himself surrounded by naked slaves smeared with honey so that a biting flies would be attracted to them and not bite him.

Ivan the Terrible blinded the two architects who designed his new church of Saint Basil's so that they could never make anything more beautiful.

Mongolian leader Tamerlane played polo using the skulls of enemies killed in battle.

The Russian ruler Peter the Great had his wife's lover decapitated and insisted that she keep his head in a jar of alcohol beside her bed as a reminder of her crime.

Animal Facts

There are more than 70,000 types of slug and snail in the world. Let's hope they never hold a big party!

The pearl fish swims into a sea cucumber's anus and lives inside it in the day time, coming out at night. The sea cucumber breathes through its anus, so can't keep the fish out!

The glass frog has a transparent body — its blood vessels, stomach and beating heart are all visible.

Spiders inject flies and bugs with a chemical which paralyzes them and dissolves their insides. The spider then sucks out the liquid as it can't chew.

A scorpion can go for a whole year without eating.

As cockroaches grow, they develop a new skin inside their old one, eventually splitting the old one. This new skin is white until it hardens in the air and becomes dark.

The viperfish has teeth so long it can't close its mouth and it has to open its jaws out flat before it can swallow. Its teeth are half the length of its head!

A mosquito can drink one and a half times its own weight in blood at a single meal. Yuk!

The skin of a hippopotamus measures about 4 centimetres (1.5 inches) thick. That's about 3.5 centimetres (over an inch) thicker than human skin.

Bone-eating zombie worms live on the decaying bodies of dead whales. They have no gut, but bore deeply into the bones. Microbes inside the worms digest chemicals sucked out of the bones.

The banded tenrec, a kind of hedgehog from Madagascar, sometimes eats so many worms, bugs and slugs that it makes itself sick.

Sharks will eat almost anything. The stomachs of dead sharks have been found to contain bits of boats and vehicles and even a knight in armour.

If a rat didn't keep chewing, its lower teeth would eventually grow through its top jaw and up into the roof of its mouth.

A shark can taste blood over a kilometre (about half a mile) away.

A spider that isn't hungry will wrap up extra bugs in its web to keep for later.

In the time of the dinosaurs, there were giant scorpions nearly a metre (3 feet) long. That's bigger than the average domestic dog!

Every year, 4.5 million litres (1 million gallons) of dog urine goes into the parks of London, England.

There are 3,500 known species of cockroach. Are there others out there? We just don't know yet...

Owl's eyes are too large to move in their eye sockets, so they've developed the ability to turn their heads round further than other birds can.

Salamander larvae change form, becoming killer predators, if they sense the vibrations created in water by swimming tadpoles. They grow longer, stronger bodies and broader heads so that they can kill and eat the tadpoles.

A planarian worm will regrow its other half it cut in two. If two planarians are cut in half, they can be mixed up and re-attach to the wrong half.

Flesh flies eat nothing but old meat and rotting flesh on dead bodies.

The vampire squid has the largest eyes of any animal for its body size. The squid is 28 centimetres long (11 inches) and its eyes are 2.5 centimetres (1 inch across). The equivalent would be a person with eyes the size of table tennis bats!

A duck-billed platypus can stuff its cheek pouches with 600 worms.

Geckos have no eyelids – they lick their eyeballs to clean them!

The job of guard termites is to defend the termite nest or mound. Sometimes they explode in their efforts to deter attackers.

Scorpions glow in the dark in ultraviolet light.

A lion's mane jellyfish is about 2.5 metres (8 feet) across, with tentacles 60 metres (200 feet) long. Their sting can cause an agonizing death.

An octopus has to turn itself inside out to eat, as its mouth is hidden in between its tentacles.

The leopard seal sometimes attacks people, lunging up through the ice to snap at their feet.

The southern giant petrel, a bird which lives near the South Pole, spits globs of oil and regurgitated food at its enemies.

The carpet viper kills more people in the world than any other type of snake. Its bite leads to uncontrollable bleeding.

A baby naked mole rat has transparent skin – you can see its insides right through its skin!

Cockroaches taste through their feet.

Copepods are tiny crustaceans that swim around in groups of up to a trillion. They are the only known creature that has just one eye.

The wood frog that lives in the Arctic Circle can stay deep-frozen for weeks and survive.

> **Horses often chew at fly eggs and maggots on their legs and end up swallowing them, so have a stomach full of crawling maggots.**

Nose bots are maggots that live inside the noses of animals that graze, such as sheep, cows and horses.

> **The Gila monster is a lizard from South America and Mexico. Although it's only just over half a metre (2 feet) long, its bite is so strong that the only way to detach one that's bitten you is to drown it.**

A rat can fall from a five-storey building and walk away unharmed.

Rats have super-strong teeth. Amongst other things, they can bite through wood, metal and electric cables.

A cockroach can survive being frozen in a block of ice for two days.

The only mammals that don't get lice are anteaters, armadillos, bats, duck-billed platypuses, whales, dolphins and porpoises.

The deep-sea gulper eel can eat fish larger than itself. It can open its mouth so wide that its jaw bends back on itself at an angle of more than 180 degrees.

The caterpillar of the polyphemus moth in North America eats 86,000 times its own birthweight in the first 56 days of its life. It's equal to a human baby eating 270 tonnes (nearly 600,000 pounds) of food!

Geckos have transparent eyelids which are permanently closed but allow the gecko to see anyway.

The bulldog ant from Australia will sting again and again while holding on with its fierce jaws. It can kill a human in 15 minutes.

A pregnant scorpion will sometimes reabsorb its babies instead of giving birth to them.

Chameleons can change their skin colour to hide themselves (camouflage) – but they also change colour according to mood. Some go grey when depressed.

Mosquitoes in the Arctic hatch when the snows thaw, sometimes making such large swarms they blot out the sun.

Head lice suck blood for about 45 seconds every 2–3 hours, but they can go without a meal for up to two days if they are between heads – on a comb, towel or pillow.

A kind of yellow-bellied toad can produce a nasty foam that smells of garlic to deter attackers.

The naked mole rat is perhaps the ugliest mammal in the world. It looks like a wrinkly sausage with very short legs and huge, protruding teeth. It has no hair anywhere except the inside of its mouth.

The bluebottle nd greenbottle flies non in houses lay their s in rotting meat, dead animals and animal faeces.

Komodo dragons are lizards 3 metres (10 feet) long. They aren't poisonous, but there are so many bacteria in their mouths – growing in rotten meat between their teeth – that a bite from one often leads to blood poisoning and death.

Bracken Cave in Texas is home to 20 million bats. The floor is caked in a thick layer of bat faeces.

Only female mosquitoes bite and suck blood – they need the protein in blood so that they can lay eggs. The males only eat nectar from flowers.

Crows are one of the few larger creatures that will eat rotting and putrid flesh.

A maggot doesn't have teeth – it oozes a kind of spit called *ferment* onto its food. This dissolves the food, and the maggot then sucks it up.

The axolotl is a pale amphibian that is part way between a tadpole and a lizard, and lives in a single lake in Mexico. Some axolotls change shape and become land creatures, but most don't ever change.

A hissing cockroach makes a noise by squeezing air out of tiny holes in its body segments. The sound can be heard 3.7 metres (12 feet) away.

An octopus tentacle will carry on wriggling for some time after being cut off.

Baby Komodo dragons will eat their brothers and sisters if they are hungry and there is no other food.

If an octopus loses a tentacle it can grow a new one.

A sting-ray has a special cap on the end of its tail which breaks off when it stings, allowing poison to pour out into the wound it's made in its victim.

The aye-aye is a nocturnal mammal from Madagascar that has one very long, bony finger on one hand. It looks so frightening that local people believed contact with an aye-aye led to death, so they killed most of them.

Bat faeces lies so deep on the floors of their caves that people harvest it to sell as fertilizer for plants.

Mosquitoes have been around for 200 million years. That's so long that even dinosaurs could have been bitten by them!

The guanay cormorant makes its nest from dried faeces.

Flies beat their wings about 180 times a second.

The angler fish has a glowing blob attached to a spike at the front of its head. In the dark, deep sea the glowing blob attracts small prey which the angler fish then sucks in and gobbles up.

Electric eels can deliver a shock of 500 volts to stun their dinner into submission.

Flies eat by vomiting up something they've eaten previously so that the chemicals in their vomit can start to dissolve the new meal. When it's sloppy, they suck it all up again. That's why it's a really bad idea to eat anything a fly's been sitting on!

Sharks have special organs in their snouts and elsewhere that let them detect the electric fields produced by living animals. They can then home in on the animals to eat them.

The face fly feeds on the mucus produced in a cow's eyes and nostrils.

A giraffe has special valves in its arteries so that its blood can reach up to its head. Without them, it would need a heart as big as its whole body!

A cockroach can withstand more than 120 times the force of the Earth's gravity – an astronaut passes out at 12 times the pressure of gravity.

Plagues of flying foxes (fruit bats) can destroy a fruit orchard in a single night.

Land leeches in Asia can drop from trees onto people and suck out so much blood the person dies.

Slugs are attracted to beer; some gardeners trap them by putting out bowls of beer which the slugs fall into. They get drunk and drown. The slugs, not the gardeners!

Goliath bird-eating spiders can grow to the size of a dinner plate and kill small birds.

A 32-kilogram (70-pound) octopus can squeeze through a hole the size of a tennis ball.

The end of a chameleon's tongue can have a club-like lump oiled with sticky goo which helps it to catch insects.

The Australian blue-ringed octopus can pump out a poison that will paralyze or kill a human.

Some toads can swallow shrews and mice whole.

When there's not much food around, cockroaches will eat each other – ripping open the victim's stomach and tearing out the insides.

Geckos and centipedes both eat cockroaches.

A head louse can lay 200–300 eggs during its life of around thirty days. The eggs only take five to ten days to hatch and start feeding.

Over 100 million years ago, crocodiles were twice the size they are now – up to 12 metres (40 feet) long – and could eat dinosaurs.

Baby cockroaches feed on their parents' faeces to get the bacteria they need to help them digest plants and vegetables.

The deadly box jellyfish that lives off the coast of Australia is the size of a basketball but has tentacles that trail 4.5 metres (15 feet). If the tentacles touch you, tiny harpoons inject poison.

A full-grown python can swallow a pig whole.

Rabbits partially digest the grass they eat and then excrete it as soft, gluey pellets. They then eat these to finish digesting their meal properly.

If a lizard loses its tail, it can grow a new one.

A patch of rainforest soil around the size of this book can hatch 10,000 mosquito eggs.

The geographic tree frog can change its eyes from brown to patterned to help it camouflage itself in trees.

Crocodiles carry their young around in their mouths.

When a viper fish wants to eat a large meal, it moves all its internal organs towards its tail to make more room inside it for food.

An elephant produces 23 kilograms (50 pounds) of faeces every day.

Cat urine glows in the dark (but it has to be very dark, if you're thinking of testing it).

Vampire bats drink half their body weight in blood every day.

Light-coloured spots on surfaces of food show a fly has vomited something up and tasted the surface; dark-coloured spots are fly faeces.

A ribbon worm can eat 95 percent of its own body and still survive.

A cockroach can live for a week after its head is cut off.

When a fish called the Pacific grenadier is pulled out of the sea by fishermen, the change in pressure makes gas inside it expand quickly and its stomach pops out of its mouth.

A vampire finch in the Galapagos Islands pecks holes in other birds to feed on their blood.

Dogs in New York, USA, produce 18 million kilograms (40 million pounds) of faeces a year. Luckily, New Yorkers have to clear up after their dogs.

A leech will suck blood until it is ten times its original size and can't hold any more. Once it's full, it drops off its victim.

Leeches don't only suck from the outside of your body. If you drink water with a leech in, it can attach to the inside of your mouth or throat and, in a river, leeches can go into your bottom and suck you from the inside.

The gavial, a kind of crocodile from India, has over a hundred teeth.

The potato beetle larva protects itself from birds that want to eat it by covering itself in its own poisonous faeces.

When a toad is sick, it vomits up its own stomach, which hangs out of its mouth for a short time before it swallows it back down.

The turkey vulture excretes faeces onto its legs to keep them cool.

A chameleon's tongue can be twice as long as its body, and must be kept curled to fit inside it.

A baby robin eats 4 metres (14 feet) of earthworms a day!

The female black widow spider eats the male after mating, sometimes eating up to twenty-five partners a day. Now *that's* a man-eater!

Many leeches produce a pain-killer so that you don't notice you have been bitten unless you actually see the leech.

A very stressed octopus will sometimes eat itself.

The queen naked mole rat is the only one to have babies. She keeps the others sterile (incapable of having babies) using a special chemical in her urine.

A female German cockroach can produce 500,000 young in a year.

Crocodiles can't bite and chew. Instead, they hold their prey under water to drown it, then twist their bodies around to tear chunks off the victim.

Body lice love dirty places – they were very common in the old days when people didn't wash much, and they often infested soldiers who had to live in dirty conditions. They are most likely to live on your tummy or your bottom.

World Record Facts

Charles Osbourne, from Iowa, USA, hiccupped every 1.5 seconds for 69 years and then suddenly stopped.

The most expensive coffee in the world is made with coffee beans recovered from the faeces of the civet, a type of wild cat from Sumatra.

At a single meal, obese New Yorker Walter Hudson could eat:
12 doughnuts,
10 packets of crisps,
8 Chinese take-aways
and half a cake!

Peter Dowdeswell of the UK ate a three-course meal in a record 45 seconds in 1999. He ate oxtail soup, mashed potatoes, baked beans and sausage, and then prunes.

Natasha Verushka of the USA holds the record for sword-swallowing; she swallowed 13 swords at a convention in 2004.

> **The biggest cockroach in the world is the Madagascan hissing cockroach. It can grow to 9 centimetres (3.5 inches) – as long as an adult's finger.**

Monte Pierce of the USA can flick a coin 3.3 metres (10 feet 10 inches) with his earlobes.

The black-headed sea snake found north of Australia in the Timor Sea is 100 times more deadly than the most poisonous snake on land.

Leonardo d'Andrea from Italy smashed 32 watermelons with his head in 1 minute in 2005.

Marc Quinquandon, from France, set a world record by eating 144 snails in 11 minutes. He beat his own record when he ate 72 snails in 3 minutes, but he died soon afterwards.

In 2005, Matthew Henshaw from Australia swallowed a sword 40.5 centimetres (15.9 inches) long, and hung a sack of potatoes weighing 20 kilograms (44 pounds 5 ounces) on its handle for 5 seconds.

The loudest recorded scream was 129 decibels, made by Jill Drake of the UK at a Halloween celebration in 2000.

The biggest beetle in the world is the dung-eating Goliath beetle – it's about the size of a hamster!

In 1998, 13 year-old Daniel Canal of Miami, USA, received 12 transplanted organs in only 3 weeks.

By March 2005, American Donald Gorske had eaten 20,500 Big Macs. He has eaten at least one a day for 33 years.

Gordon Cates of the USA holds the record for kissing poisonous snakes. He kissed 11 cobras in 1999.

A woman who worked on smelly feet in a testing laboratory had to smell 5,600 feet over 15 years.

A Japanese woman holds the record for having most worms removed from her stomach; doctors removed a total of 56 in 1990.

Tom Shufflebottham charmed 511 worms out of the ground at a worm-charming championship in England in 1980.

Norman Gary of the USA held 109 live honey bees in his mouth for 10 seconds in 1998.

In 1997, an Egyptian boy of 16 was found to have his unborn identical twin growing inside him. It had died at about 32–33 weeks old and was 45 centimetres (18 inches) long.

Michael Lloyd of the USA holds the record for kicking himself in the head – 42 times in a row!

Danny Capps holds the record for spitting a dead cricket out of his mouth, reaching a distance of 9.17 metres (30 feet).

Hu Saelao of Thailand has not cut his hair for more than 70 years.

Ken Edwards of the UK ate 36 live cockroaches in one minute on a breakfast TV show in 2001.

The two smelliest substances are gross gases which the US government is investigating as possible weapons. They would be used to break up crowds without harming people. One is called 'Who Me?' and the other 'The US Government Standard Bathroom Malodor'.

Ciro Gallo of the UK holds the record for having concrete blocks broken on his chest with a sledge hammer, while lying on a bed of nails – 37 blocks weighing a total of 235.8 kilograms (519.8 pounds).

The longest-lasting operation took 96 hours and was carried out in Chicago, USA, in 1951 to remove a giant tumour.

Dustin Phillips of the USA can drink a whole bottle of tomato ketchup through a straw in only 33 seconds.

In 1999, American Scott Jeckel shot a marshmallow 4.96 metres (16.27 feet) out of his nose, with his friend Ray Perisin catching it in his mouth.

Shridhar Chillal grew his fingernails for 44 years without cutting them. Their average length was 117 centimetres (46 inches), and his thumbnail was 132 centimetres (52 inches).

Robert Earl Hughes of Illinois, USA had the largest chest measurement ever recorded. He was 3.15 metres (10 feet 4 inches) around the chest when he died, aged 32. He weighed 484 kilograms (1,067 pounds).

> **In 1976, American Jon Brower Minoch weighed 635 kilograms (1,400 pounds). He was so fat that it took 12 firemen to lift him out of his house when he fell ill, and 13 nurses to turn him over in bed. In fact, he had two beds strapped together as one wasn't big enough to hold him. He once put on 89 kilograms (196 pounds) in a single week.**

The smallest fully-grown adult ever to live was Gul Mohammed of India, who was 57 centimetres (34.5 inches) tall at the age of 33 and weighed only 17 kilograms (37.5 pounds).

The record for spitting a mouthful of tobacco is 16.23 metres (53 feet 3 inches), set in 1997.

The longest recorded eyebrow hair was 7.8 centimetres (3.1 inches) long.

The most poisonous fish in the world is the stone fish. Treading on its spines causes a painful death in 20 minutes.

The worst epidemic of all time was the Black Death – a plague carried by fleas that live on rats – which killed 75 million people in Europe and Asia between 1347 and 1351.

A hairball weighing 2.53 kilograms (5 pounds 3 ounces) was removed from the stomach of a 20 year-old English woman in 1895.

The largest ever kidney stone – a solid mass of mineral that collects inside the kidneys – weighed 356 grams (12.5 ounces). It was removed from a man in Australia in 2003.

The longest leg hair grew on Australian man Tim Stinton – it was 12.4 centimetres (4.9 inches) long.

The winner of a fly-swatting contest in 1912 killed 543,360 flies, weighing a total of 96 kilograms (212 pounds).

Kim Goodman from the USA can 'bob' her eyeballs out of their sockets so that they stick out 11 millimetres (0.4 inches).

Motorcycle stunt rider Evel Knievel of Montana, USA, holds the record for broken bones – he suffered 435 fractures while working as stunt rider.

Thomas Wedders, who lived in England in the 1770s, is said to have had a nose 19 centimetres (7.5 inches) long.

The youngest person to have a full set of false teeth was only 4 years old. He suffered from an inherited disease that destroyed his teeth.

American Robert Wadlow had the largest feet ever recorded. They were 47 centimetres (18.5 inches) long.

Garry Turner of the UK can stretch a flap of skin away from his body to a length of 15.8 centimetres (6.25 inches). He has a medical condition that affects his skin making it super-elastic.

Monte Pierce from the USA can stretch his left ear lobe to a length of 12.7 centimetres (5 inches).

Stephen Taylor from the UK can stick his tongue out 9.4 centimetres (3.7 inches) measured from the tip to his lips.

The longest beard ever was grown by Hans Langseth of Norway, whose whiskers stretched an incredible 5.33 metres (17.6 inches) when measured on his death in Kensett, Iowa, in 1927. The beard was presented to the Smithsonian Institution, Washington DC, in 1967.

Rene Alvarenga of El Salvador has eaten 35,000 live scorpions. He catches them himself with his bare hands and eats 20 to 30 per day.

Shamsher Singh from India has the longest beard on a living man. In 1997, it was 1.83 metres (6 feet) long.

Thomas Blackthorne of the UK can lift 11 kilograms (24 pounds) of weights using just his tongue.

Giovanni Batista from Orsenigo, Italy, has a collection of more than 2 million human teeth.

Letchemanah Ramasamy from Malaysia has pulled a double-decker bus 30 metres (around 98 feet), using only his hair.

Wim Hof of the Netherlands exposed his whole body to ice for 1 hour 8 minutes using yoga and meditation to stop himself freezing.

French man Michel Lotito is called Monsieur Mangetout (Mr. Eat Everything) because since 1959 he has been snacking on all kinds of glass and metal. He's eaten a computer, 18 bicycles, an aeroplane, 6 chandeliers, 15 supermarket trolleys, 2 beds, 7 TV sets and a pair of skis. In total, he's eaten more than 9 tonnes (1,984 pounds) of metal.

Two people from the USA share the record for sitting in a bathtub with 75 live rattlesnakes.

The largest recorded snail was an Africa giant snail 39.3 centimetres (15.5 inches) long.

Mengxu of China can thread 20 needles in his mouth using just his tongue. He did it in 6 minutes and 45 seconds in 2003.

The largest tumour removed in one piece from a living person weighed 137.6 kilograms (303 pounds) and was 1 metre (3 feet across). It weighed more than the woman it was growing inside.

The loudest recorded burp was produced by Paul Hunn of the UK in 2004. It measured nearly 105 decibels – as loud as a fast underground train whizzing past!

The largest snail ever found was 39.3 centimetres (15.5 inches) long and weighed 900 grams (2 pounds).

Zafar Gill of Pakistan can lift 51.7 kilograms (113 pounds 15 ounces) of weights with a clamp attached to his right ear.

The largest rubbish tip in the world is Fresh Kills landfill, New York, USA. It is thought to contain 100 million tonnes (98 million tons) of rubbish and covers 1,200 hectares (3,000 acres).

American Gary Bashaw can mix chocolate powder and milk in his mouth and pour it out of his nose as milkshake. In 1999, he made a record-breaking 54 millilitres (1.8 ounces) of milkshake in one go.

Over a period of 40 years, American Charles Jensen had 970 operations to remove tumours (lumps), mostly from his face.

A bootlace worm washed up on the shore of Scotland in 1864 was 55 metres (180 feet) long.

Clint Hallam from New Zealand has lost the same hand (the right one) three times – in 1984 it was cut off in an accident and doctors re-attached it; it was removed again in 1989 when it got infected; a new, transplanted hand was removed in 2001 after rejection problems.

A man known as Snake Manu, from India, swallowed 200 earthworms each at least 10 centimetres (4 inches) long in 30 seconds in 2003.

The worst flu epidemic ever came in 1918 at the end of World War I. It killed 21 million people – twice as many as died in the war.

Tom Leppard from the UK has his whole body tattooed with leopard spots, the spaces between being tattooed yellow. This makes him the most tattooed person in the world.

In 1999, Brad Byers of the USA swallowed 10 swords each 68.5 centimetres (27 inches) long, and rotated them through 180 degrees in his throat.